Piano Solo

Moonlight Sonata

Piano Sonata in C♯ Minor, First Movement

by Ludwig van Beethoven

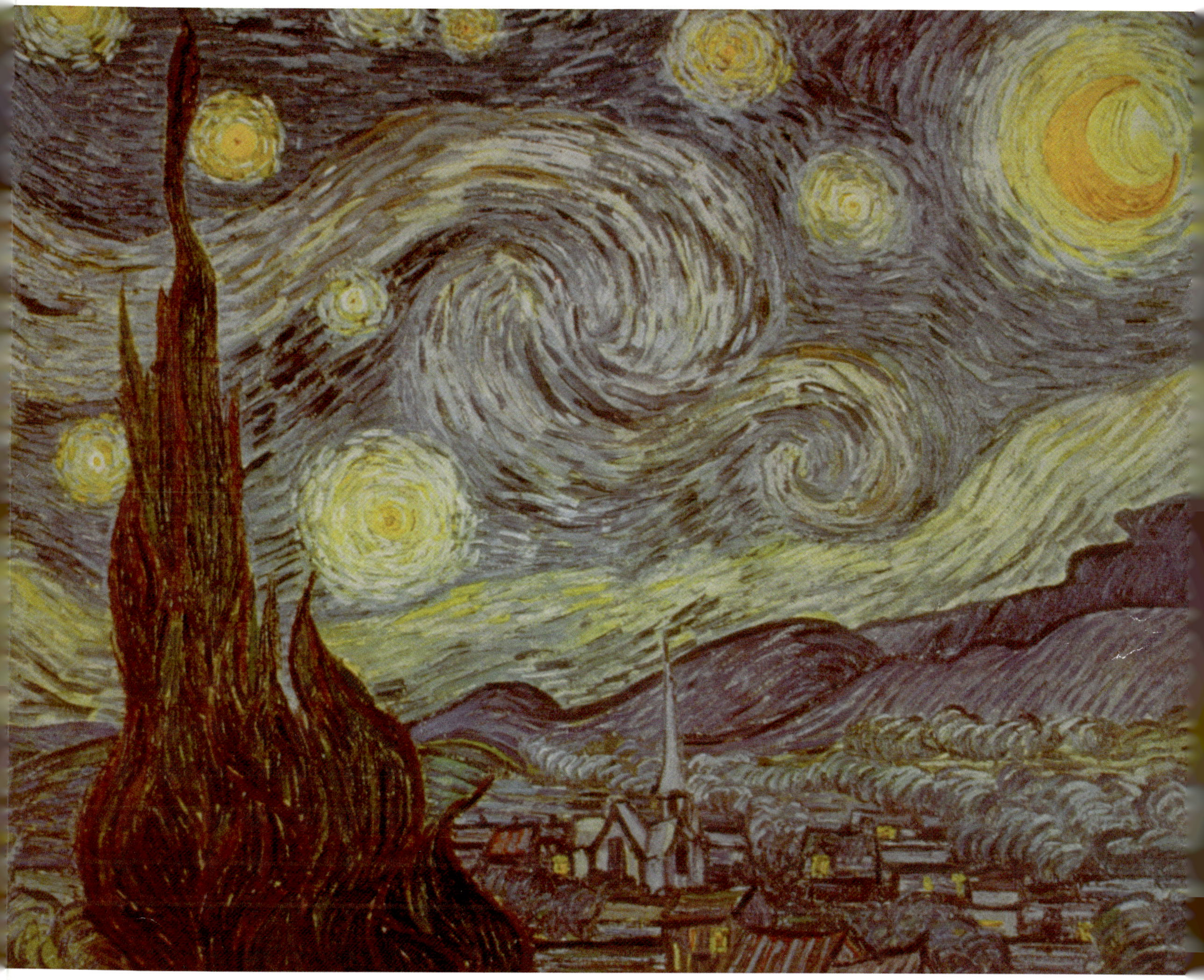

Vincent Van Gogh: *Starry Night,* 1889

PIANO SONATA NO. 14 IN C♯ MINOR

("Moonlight")

Op. 27, No. 2, First Movement

By LUDWIG VAN BEETHOVEN

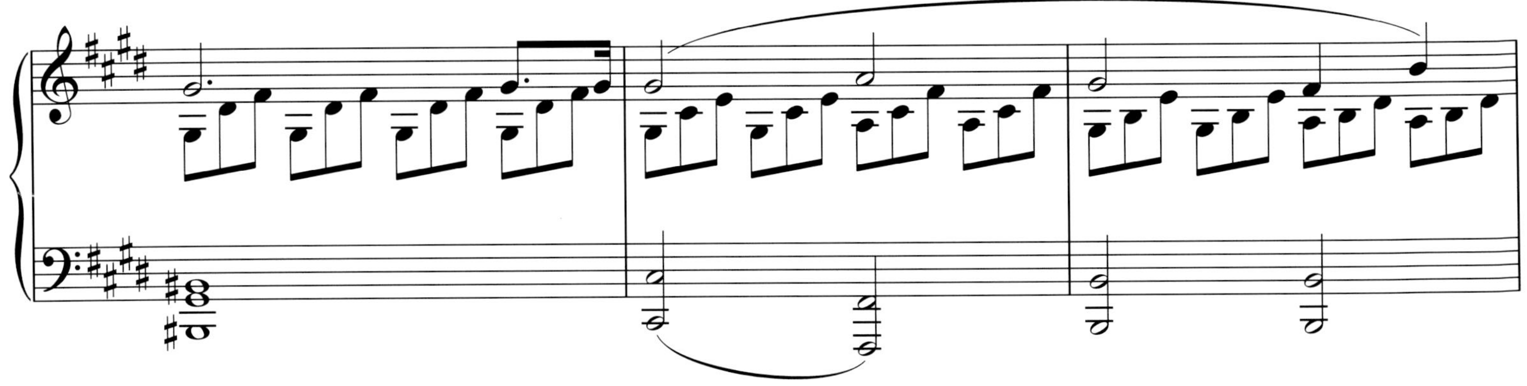

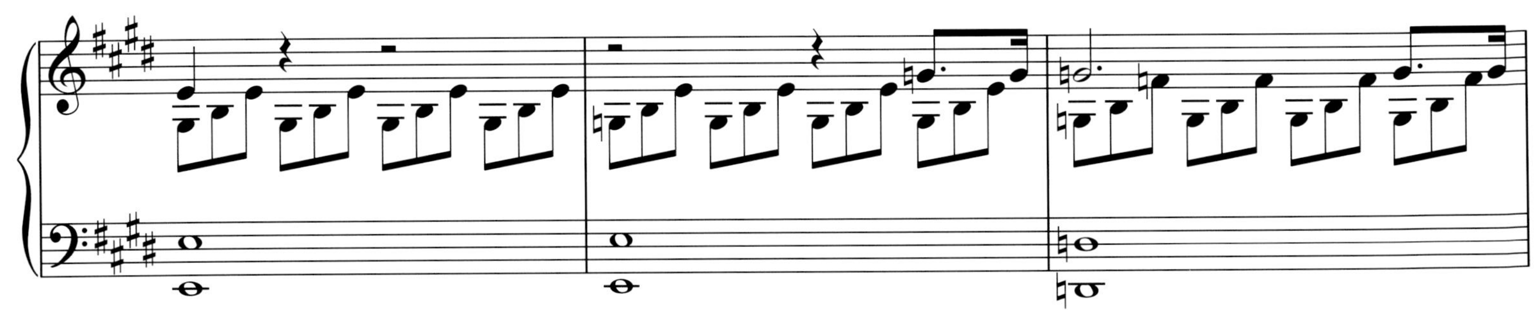

cresc.

decresc.
p
decresc.

pp
pp
cresc.

cresc.
p
pp
decresc.
pp
pp

Also available:

CLAIR DE LUNE
Piano Solo Sheet 00009417 $4.99

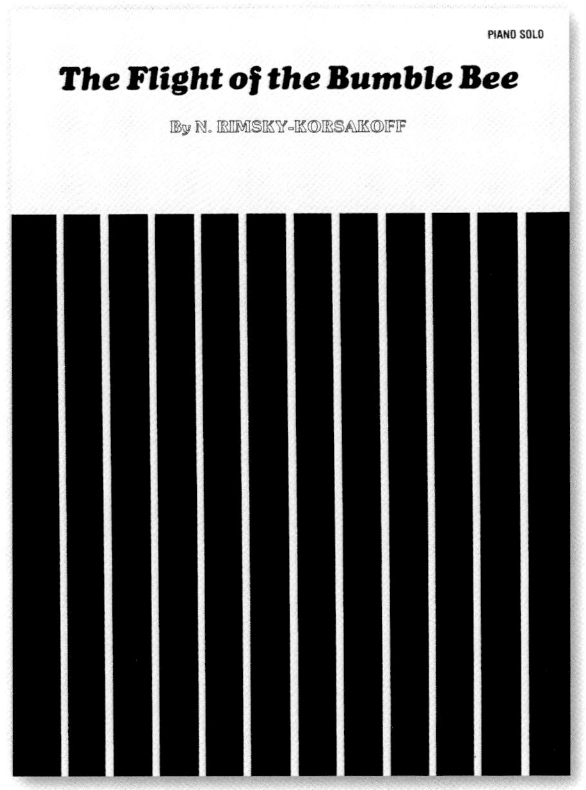

THE FLIGHT OF THE BUMBLE BEE
Piano Solo Sheet 00009427 $4.99

MALAGUEÑA
Piano Solo Sheet 00009449 $4.99

MAPLE LEAF RAG
Piano Solo Sheet 00009452 $4.99

Also available:

BEETHOVEN – FAVORITE PIANO WORKS
Piano Solo Collection 50486577 $17.99

THE BIG BOOK OF CLASSICAL MUSIC
Piano Solo Collection 00310508 $19.99

CANON IN D
Piano Solo Sheet 00202116 $4.99

FÜR ELISE
Piano Solo Sheet 00351695 $4.99

HL00351694

ISBN-13: 978-1-4950-8731-8
Distributed By
HAL LEONARD

00351694

Visit Hal Leonard Online at
www.halleonard.com

U.S. $5.99